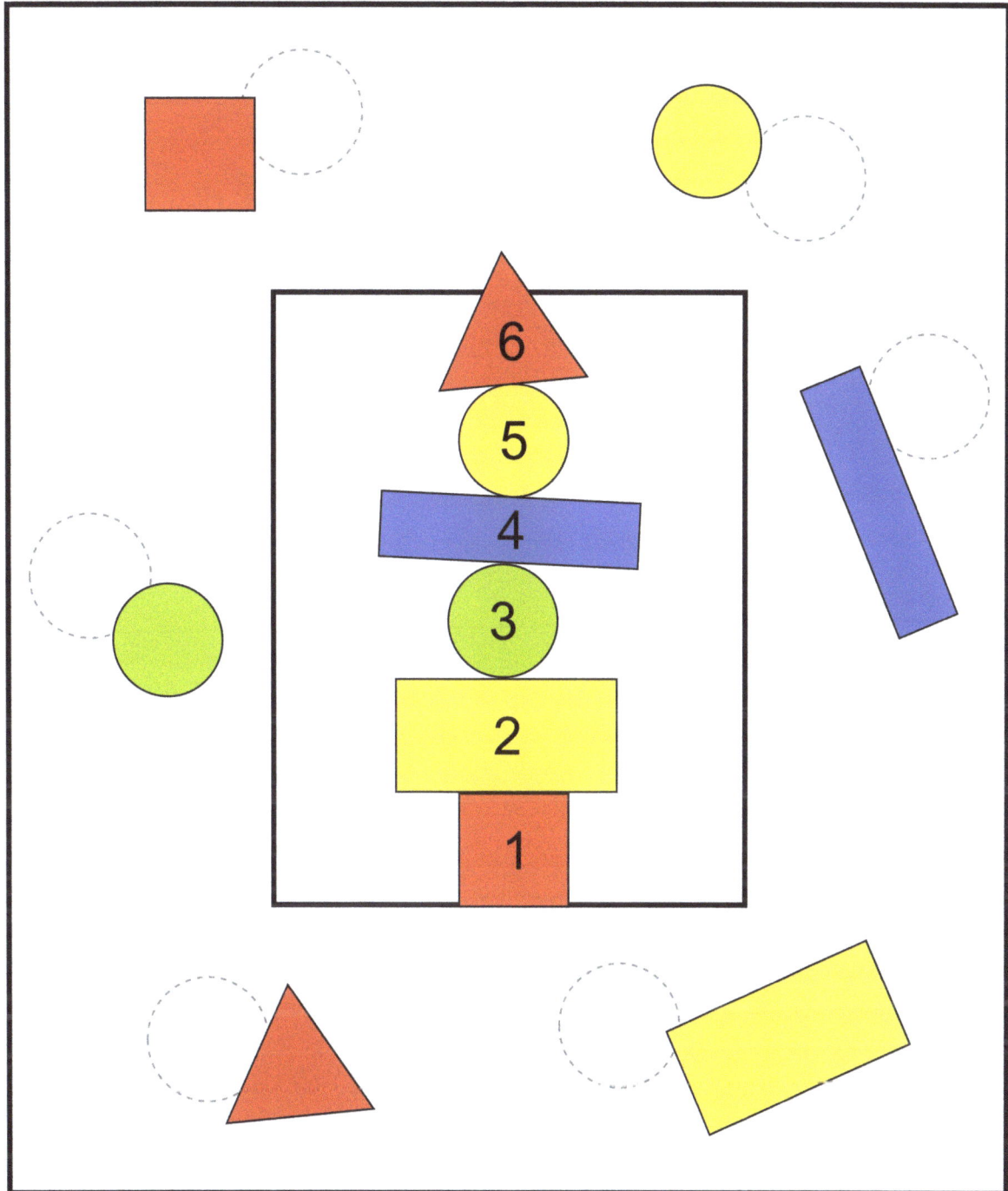

Order ALL Blocks

(Write, draw a line or use the cut-outs from the final pages.)

Super-A wants to wash her hands.
What does she need? In what order? (Use cut-outs.)

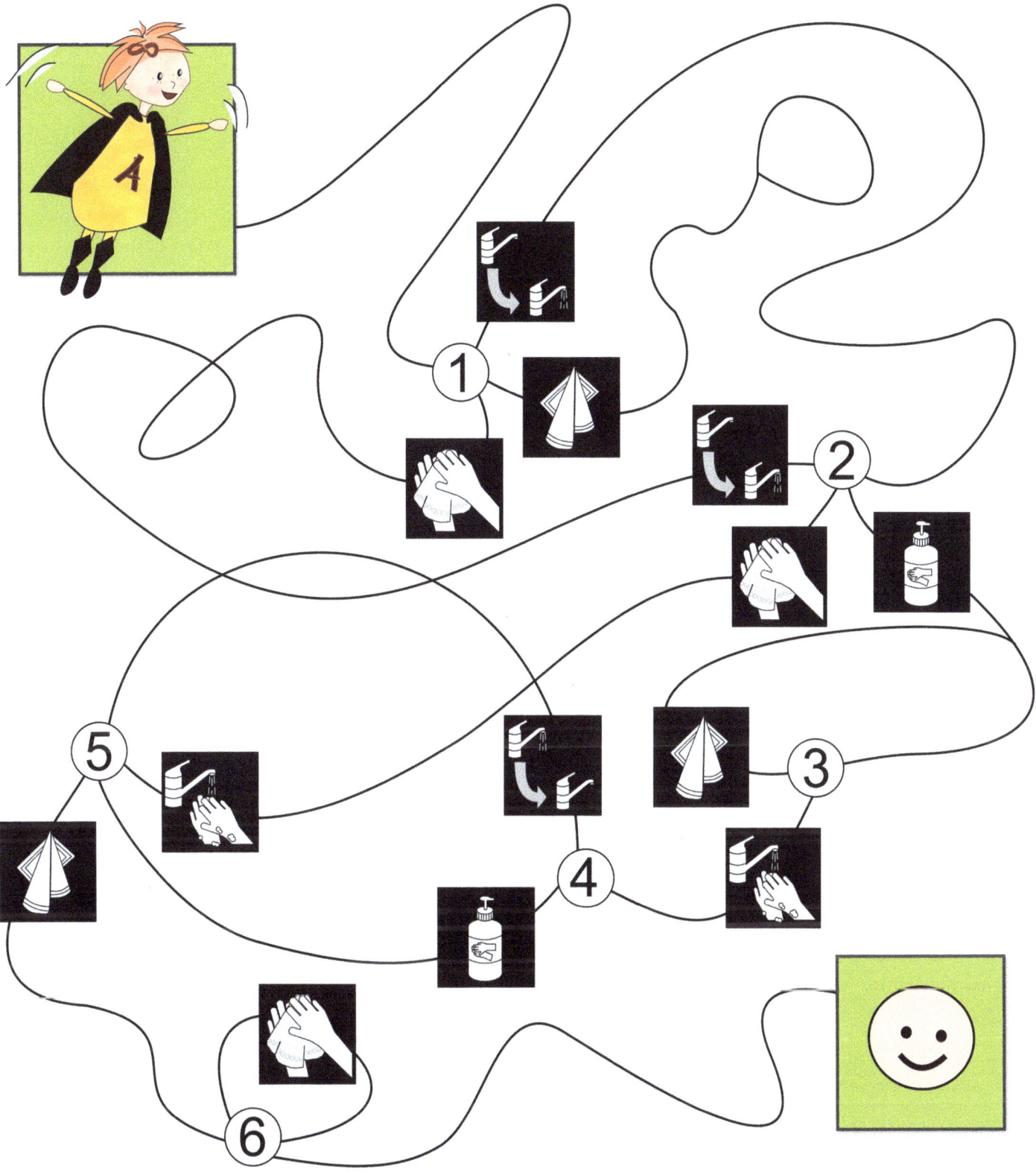

Help Super-A to wash her hands.
Find the right order!

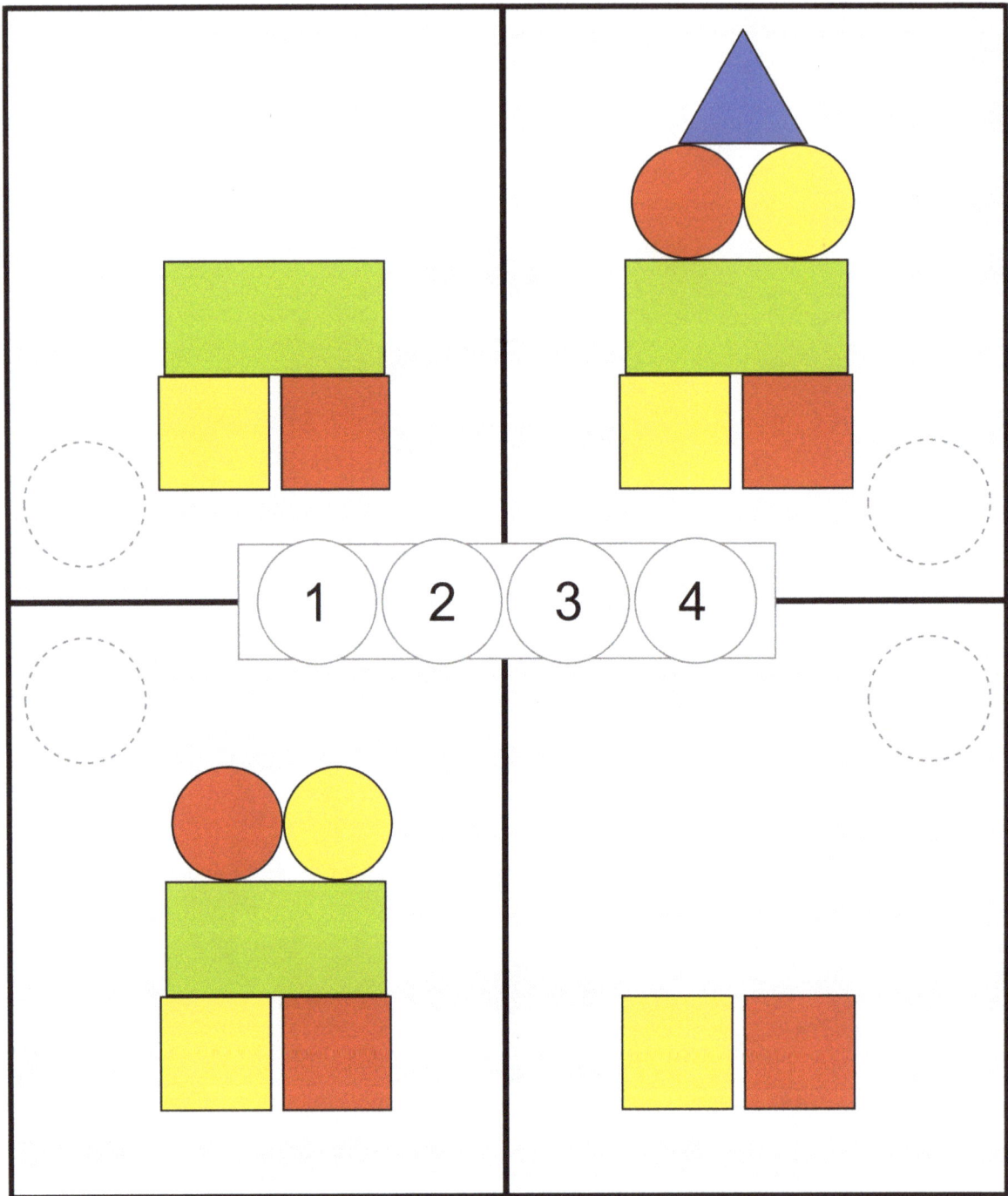

1 2 3 4

Find **RIGHT** Order

(Write, draw a line or use the cut-outs from the final pages.)

1 2 3 4

Help Adrian, Super-A and Little Miss Trigger. They all want to wash their hands. In what order is it their turn?

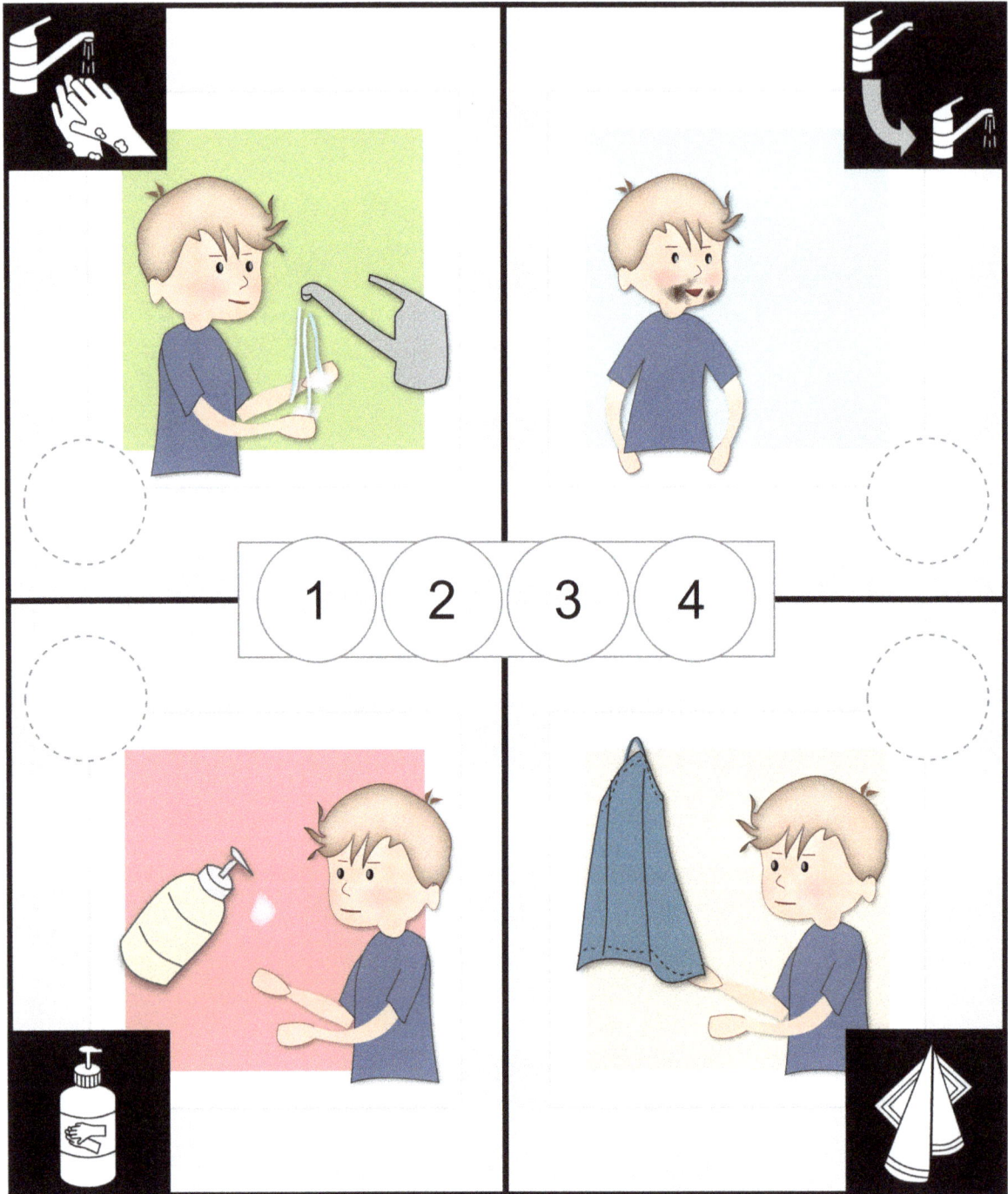

1 2 3 4

After eating cookies Adrian has to wash his hands.
Help him do everything in the right order.

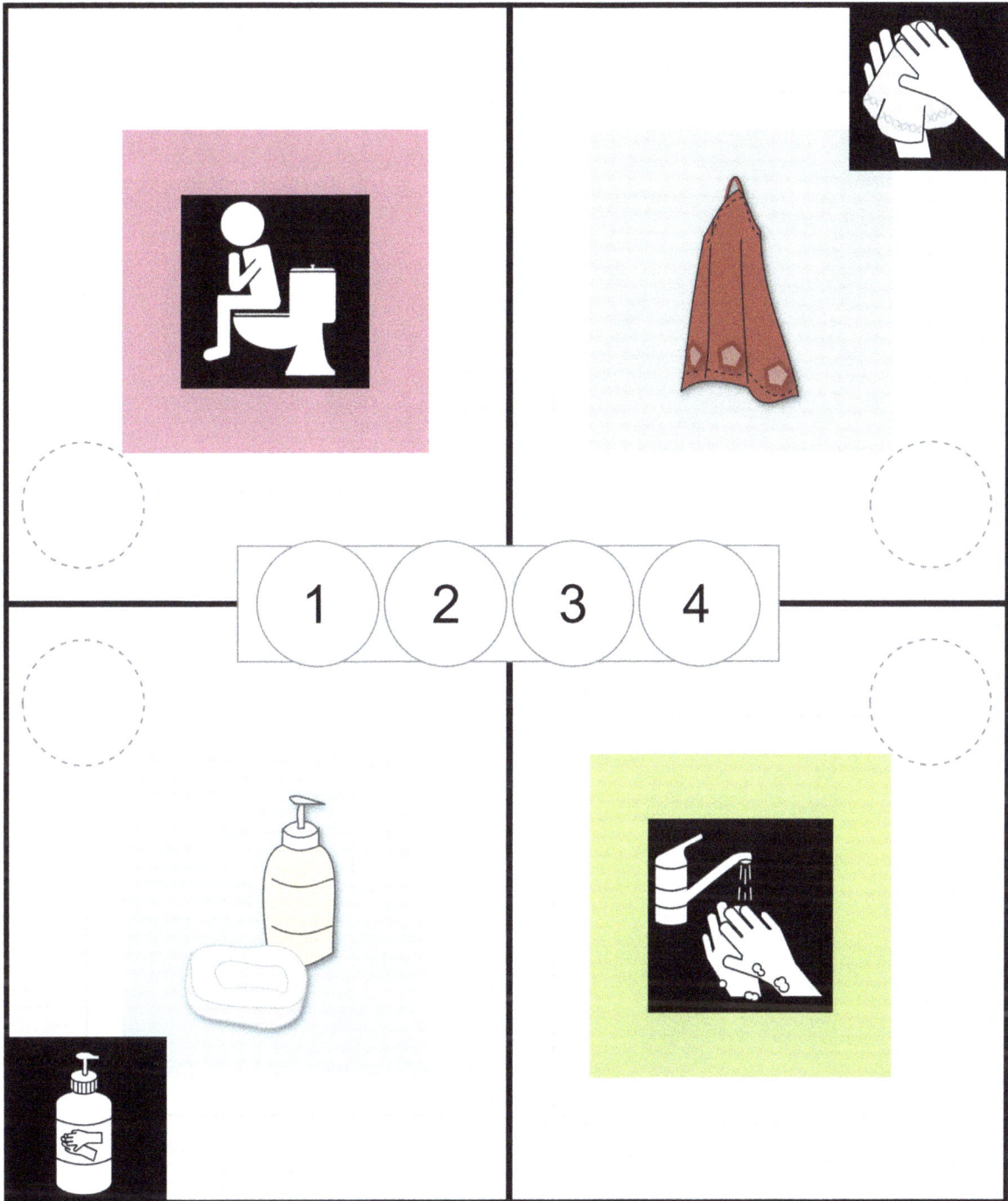

1 2 3 4

You go to the toilet. How do you wash your hands after?
Can you do everything in the right order?

Who Needs **2** Lego Bricks

Super-A played with Legos ... Adrian baked ... Mom read a book. Who has to wash hands before using the iPad?

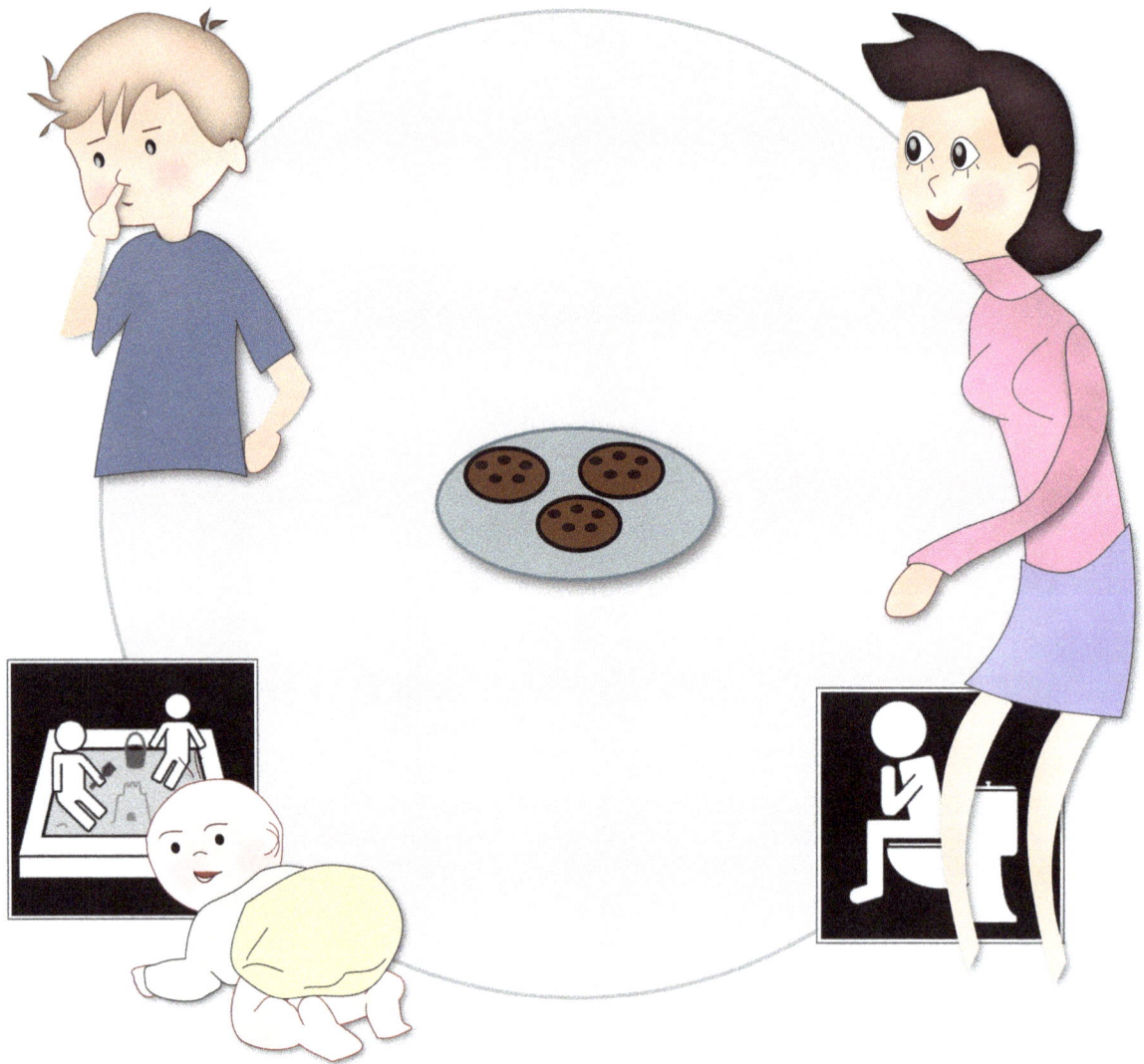

After the sandbox ... the toilet ... and picking his nose ... who has to wash hands before having cookies?

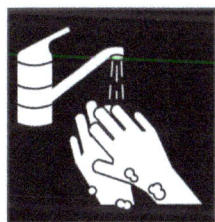

Little Brother took a bath ... Adrian ate a cookie ... and Super-A painted. Who needs to wash hands before bed?

Order **ALL** Blocks

Everybody is waiting to go outdoors.
Find a cap for each person. (Draw or use cut-outs.)

Everybody is waiting for Dad to bring a toy or a book.
Find the right toy for each person.

Everybody is waiting for something to drink.
Find a drink for each person.

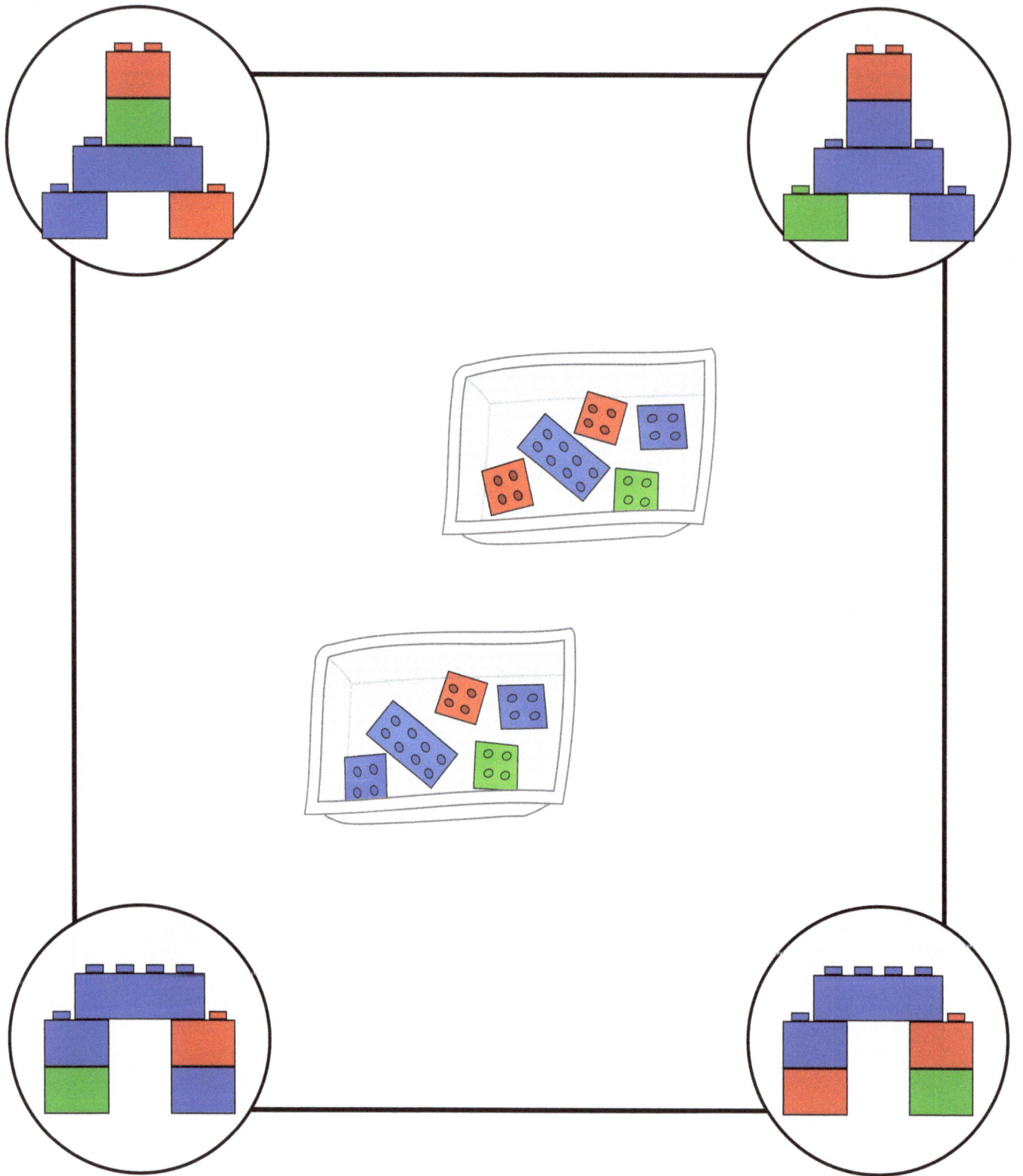

What **BOX** Builds It

Who is waiting at the table and who is not? Adrian ... Super-A ... Mom ... Little Brother ... Dad? Point to the smiley with the Wait-cap!

Who is waiting to leave the table?

Who is still eating and not waiting? Adrian ... Super-A...?

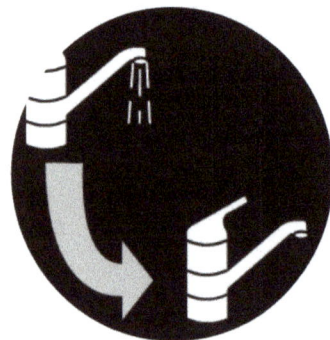

Cut out! Place the circles on the next page before playing....

Way wacky!

→

Thumbs up!

Still wet or dirty? What did they forget to use? Give Dad, Adrian, Super-A and Little Miss Trigger a circle with a towel or soap!

(Cut out the memory cards and play. Place each new pair in the correct squares above and choose a circle below.)

Who has to wait before they can ... set the table ...
... wash hands...? Place a Wait-cap on their heads.
(Use the big circles and Wait-caps on the next page.)

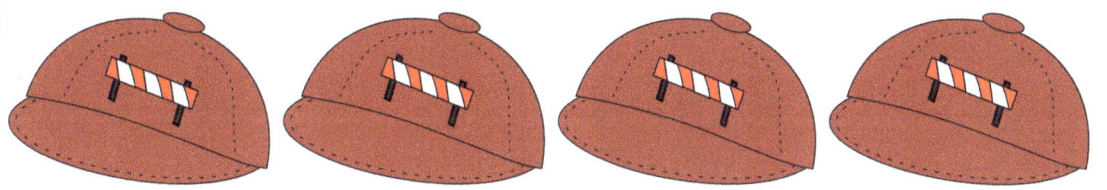

Instructions
on next page!

Instructions for the cut-outs on the previous page: The number-circles are an alternative to writing or drawing a line. They can be used in all the exercises (with dotted circles) that pair or order items. For the large circles and Wait-caps, see instructions in the last workbook exercise (and #2 below).

Want to practice more?

1) Where do we need to wait? Cut out the Wait-caps from the next page. Let your child lay out the cards in places (photos or real life) where we need to wait: hallway, table, grocery shop, lunch line, day care, in class waiting to speak, during a turn in a game, or in line to wash hands.... Who needs to wait? For what?

2) Does your child know when family members have to wait? Do they wait for the same things? Draw situations (or use photos) and place Wait-caps on family members instead of the book characters in the last workbook exercise.

     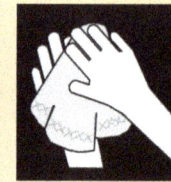

Open Tap   Take Soap   Wash with Soap   Close Tap   Take Towel   Dry Hands

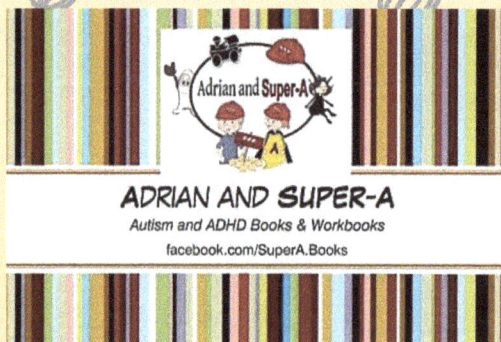

ADRIAN AND SUPER-A
Autism and ADHD Books & Workbooks
facebook.com/SuperA.Books

Be My Rails Publishing
www.BeMyRails.com

How do you want to help
your child with waiting? Use the Wait-caps
in your daily schedules with activities that require patience ...
stick the caps on a plate as a reminder to wait ... or give your
child a Wait-card to hold while you go to get something.

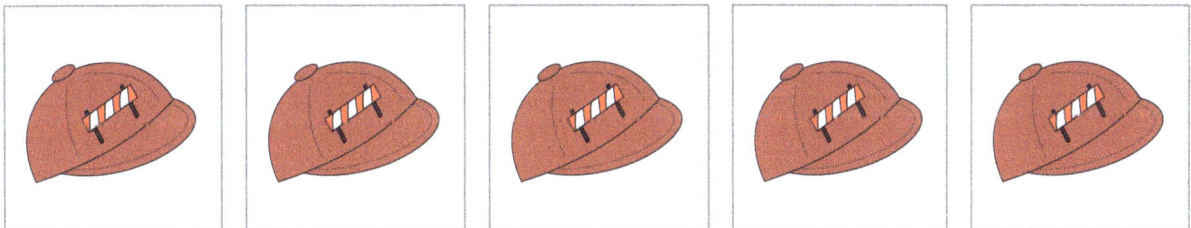

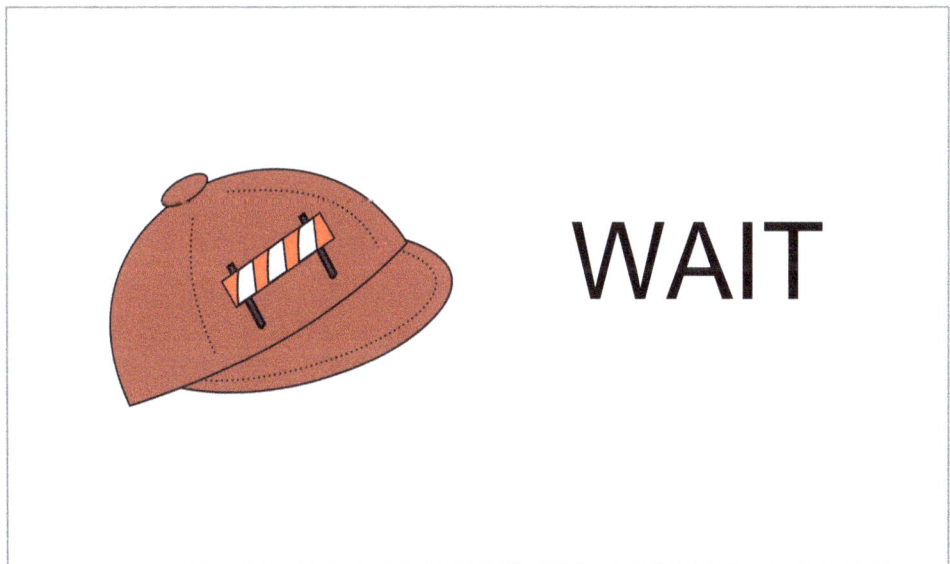

WAIT